UKULELE
CHART HITS
OF 2017-2018

ISBN 978-1-5400-2325-4

HAL•LEONARD®
7777 W. BLUEMOUND RD. P.O. BOX 13819 MILWAUKEE, WI 53213

Visit Hal Leonard Online at
www.halleonard.com

Attention

Words and Music by Charlie Puth and Jacob Hindlin

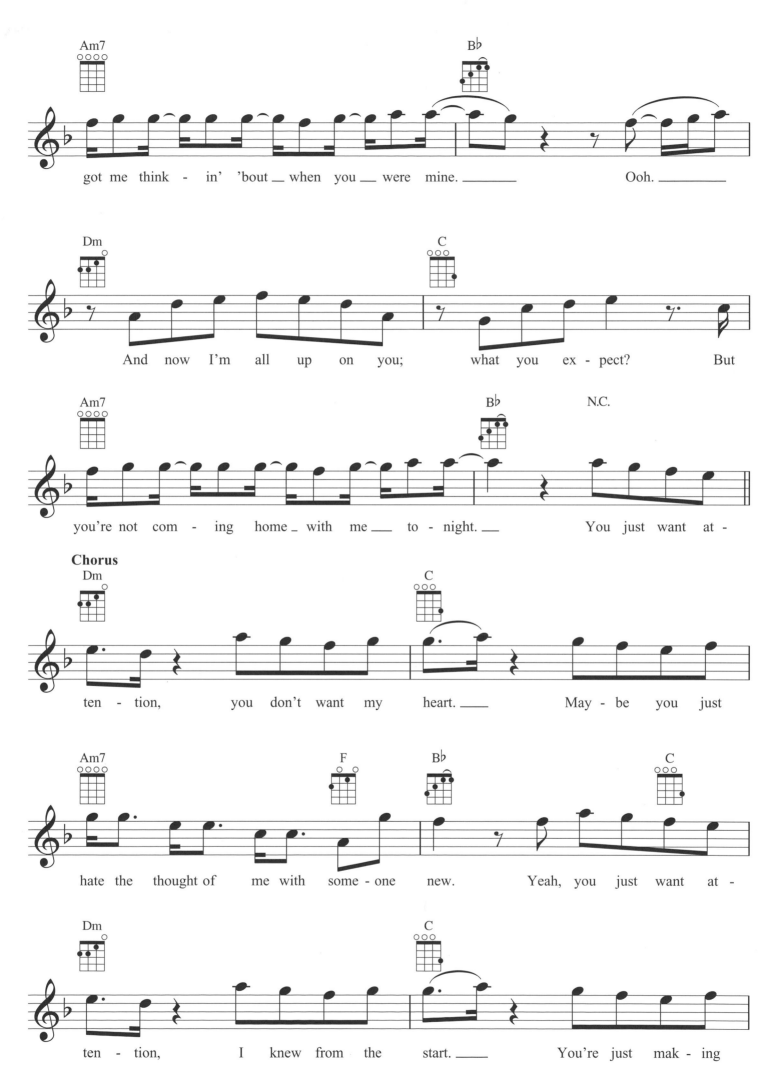

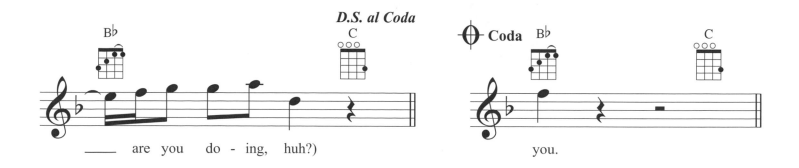

D.S. al Coda

_____ are you do - ing, huh?)

Coda

you.

Outro

(What _ are you do - ing to me? What _ are you do - ing, huh?

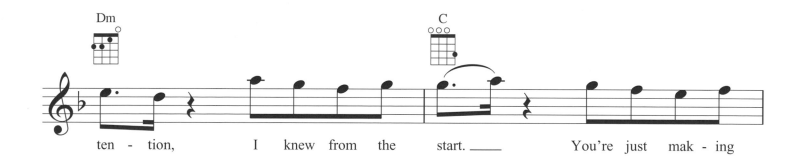

What _ are you do - ing to me? What _ are you do - ing, huh?)

Yeah, you just want at -

ten - tion, I knew from the start. _____ You're just mak - ing

sure I'm nev - er get - ting o - ver you. Oh. _____

End Game

Words and Music by Taylor Swift, Ed Sheeran,
Max Martin, Shellback and Nayvadius Wilburn

First note

Intro-Chorus 1
Moderately slow, in 2

Female: I wan - na be your end game. I wan - na be your

first string. I wan - na be your A team.

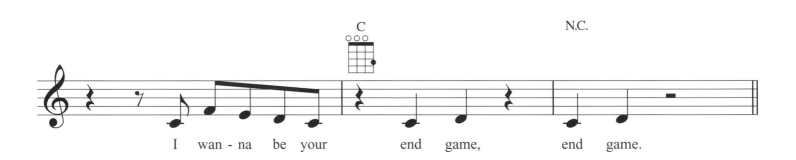

I wan - na be your end game, end game.

Chorus 2

Big rep - u - ta - tion, big rep - u - ta - tion, ooh, _____ you and me, we got
Big rep - u - ta - tion, big rep - u - ta - tion, ooh, _____ you and me would be a

bad   boy per-so-na; that's what they   like.   You love it.   I love it, too,'cause you my

type.   You hold me   down and I'll pro-tect you with my   life.   I don't wan-na

𝄋 Pre-Chorus

touch   you. (I don't wan-na   be)   just an-oth-er   ex-love (you don't wan-na
hurt   you. (I just wan-na   be)   drink-ing on the   beach with (you all o-ver

see.)   I don't wan-na   miss   you, (I don't wan-na   miss   you)   like the oth-er
me.)   I know what they   all   say, (I know what they   all   say,) but I ain't tryin' to

1., 3.   2., 4,

girls   do. _____   I don't wan-na   play. _____

Chorus 1

_____ I wan-na be your   end   game. (End   game.)   I wan-na be your

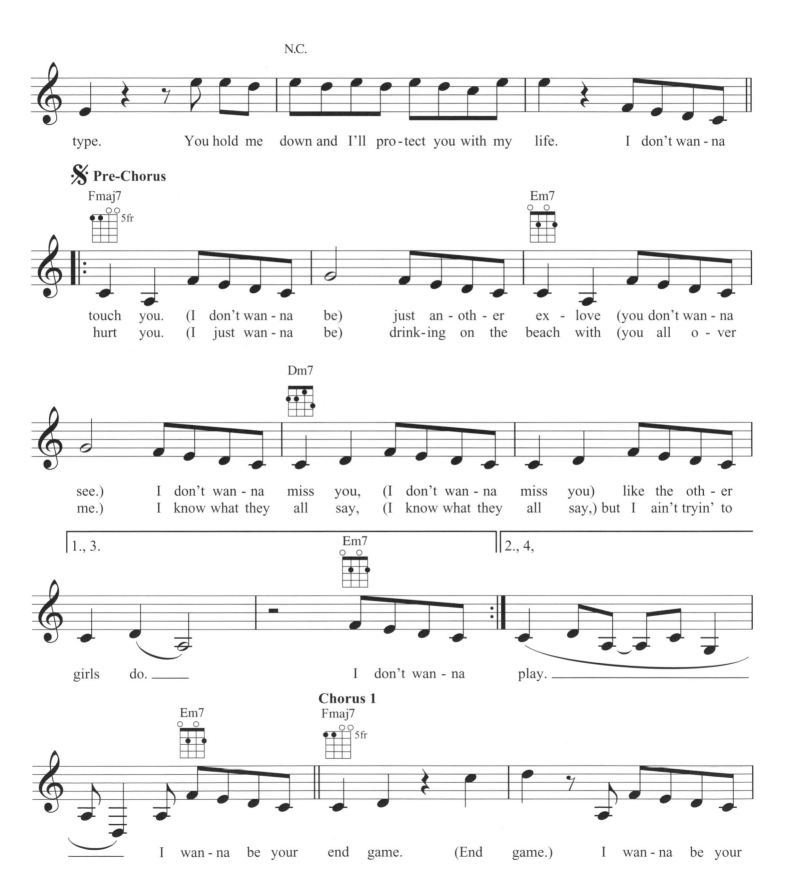

first string. (First string.) I wan-na be your A team. (A

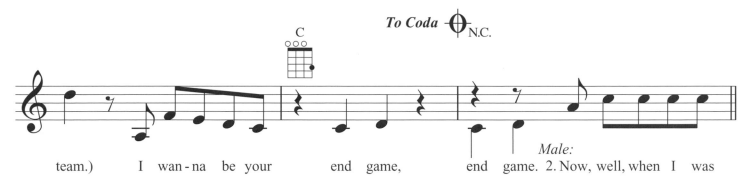

To Coda ⊕ N.C.

team.) I wan-na be your end game, end game. *Male:* 2. Now, well, when I was

Verse

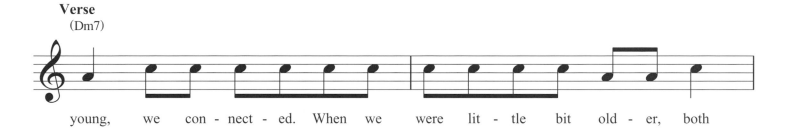

(Dm7)

young, we con-nect-ed. When we were lit-tle bit old-er, both

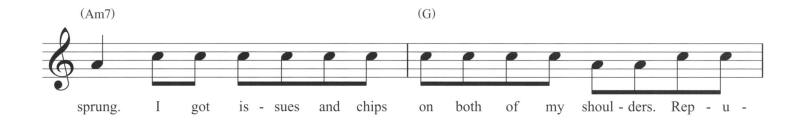

(Am7) (G)

sprung. I got is-sues and chips on both of my shoul-ders. Rep-u-

ta-tion pre-cedes __ me, and ru-mors are knee-deep. The truth is, it's eas-i-er to ig-

Dm7

nore it, be-lieve __ me. E-ven when we'd ar-gue, we'd not do it for long. And you un-der-

stand the good and bad end up in this song. For all your beau-ti-ful traits _ and the way you

do it with ease, _ for all my flaws, par-a-noi-a and in-se-cu-ri-ties. I've made mis-

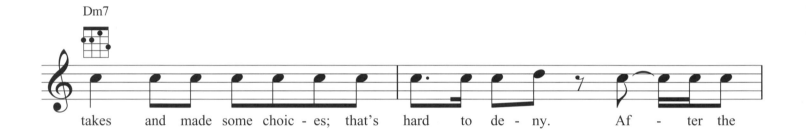

takes and made some choic-es; that's hard to de-ny. Af - ter the

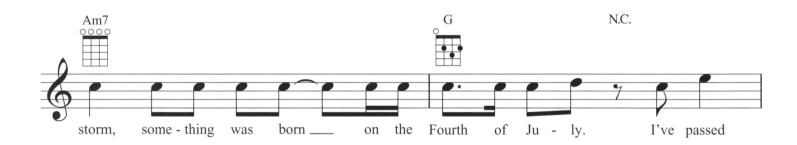

storm, some-thing was born ___ on the Fourth of Ju-ly. I've passed

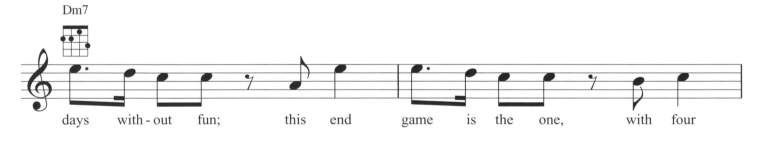

days with-out fun; this end game is the one, with four

D.S. al Coda
(with repeat)

⊕ **Coda**

Female:

words on the tip of my tongue I'll nev-er say. I don't wan-na   end game.

Chorus 2

Big rep - u - ta - tion, big rep - u - ta - tion, ooh, _____ you and me, we got
Big rep - u - ta - tion, big rep - u - ta - tion, ooh, _____ you and me would be a

big rep - u - ta - tions, ah. _____ And you heard a - bout me, ooh. __
big con - ver - sa - tion, ah. _____ And I heard a - bout you, ooh. __

1.
_____ I got some big en - e - mies.

2.
_____ You like the

Bridge

bad ones, too. *Female:* I hit you like bang. _ We tried to for - get it, but we just could - n't. And

I bur - y hatch - ets, but I keep maps of where I put 'em. Rep - u - ta - tion pre - cedes _ me; they

told you I'm cra - zy. I swear I don't love the dra - ma; it loves me. __ And I

can't let you go; __ your hand - print's on my soul. __ It's like your eyes are li - quor, it's like your

bod - y is gold. __ You've been call - ing my bluff __ on all my u - su - al tricks, __ so here's the

Outro-Chorus 1

truth from my red lips: ___ I wan - na be your end game. (End

game.) I wan - na be your first string. (First string.) I wan - na be your

A team. (A team.) I wan - na be your end game,

end game. I wan - na be your end game, end game.

Feel It Still

Words and Music by John Gourley, Zach Carothers, Jason Sechrist, Eric Howk, Kyle O'Quin, Brian Holland, Freddie Gorman, Georgia Dobbins, Robert Bateman, William Garrett, John Hill and Asa Taccone

Verse
Fast Rock

1. Can't keep my hands to my-self. ___

Think I'll dust 'em off, put 'em back up on the shelf, ___ case my

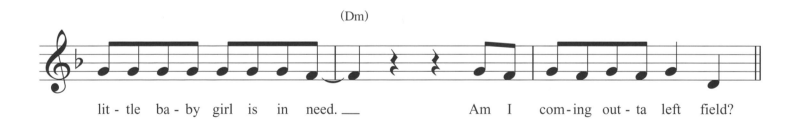

lit-tle ba-by girl is in need. ___ Am I com-ing out-ta left field?

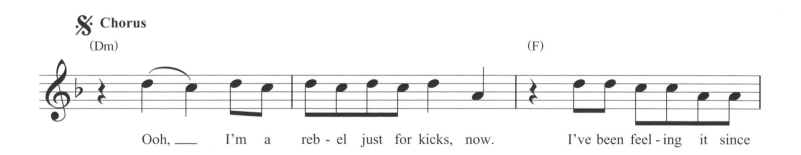

Chorus

Ooh, ___ I'm a reb-el just for kicks, now. I've been feel-ing it since

nine-teen six - ty - six, now. { Might be o - ver __ now, but I feel it still.
Might have had your _ fill, but you feel it still. }

Ooh, _____ I'm a

reb - el just for kicks, now. Let me kick it like it's nine - teen eight - y - six, now.

To Coda ⊕

Might be o - ver __ now, but I feel it still.

Verse
Dm

2. Got an - oth - er mouth to feed. _____

F   Gm

Leave it with a ba - by - sit - ter; Ma - ma, call the grave - dig - ger.

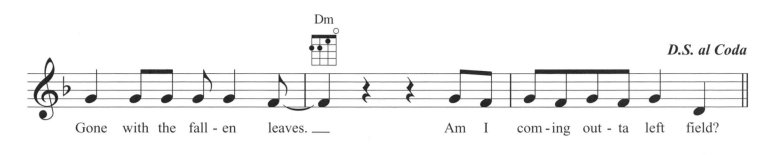

Gone with the fall-en leaves. ___ Am I com-ing out-ta left field?

Verse

Coda

3. We could fight a war for peace. ___ (Ooh, ___ I'm a

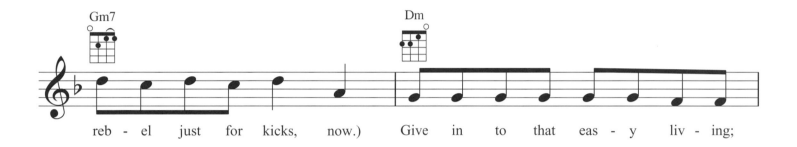

reb-el just for kicks, now.) Give in to that eas-y liv-ing;

good-bye to my hopes and dreams, ___ start

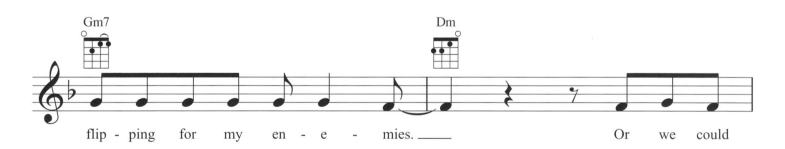

flip-ping for my en-e-mies. ___ Or we could

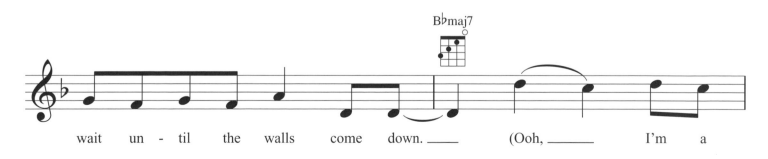

wait un-til the walls come down. ___ (Ooh, ___ I'm a

reb - el just for kicks, now.) It's time to give a lit - tle to the

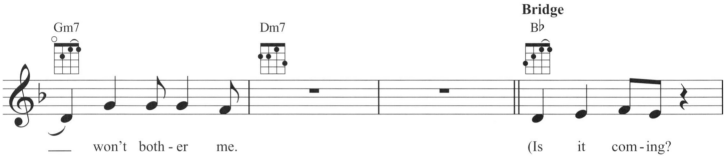

kids in the mid - dle, but, oh, _____ un - til _____ it falls, _

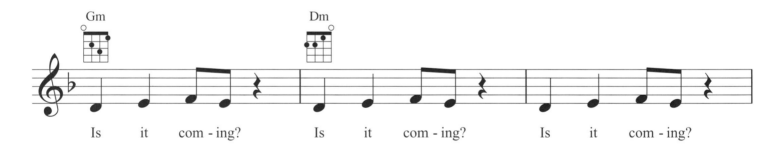

_ won't both - er me. (Is it com - ing?

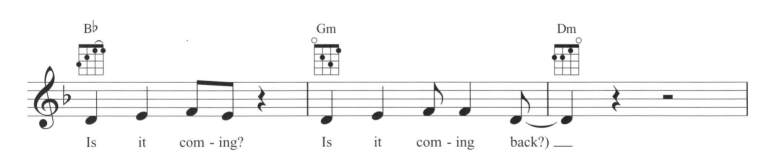

Is it com - ing? Is it com - ing? Is it com - ing?

Is it com - ing? Is it com - ing back?) _

Pre-Chorus

Ooh, _____ I'm a reb - el just for kicks. Yeah, your

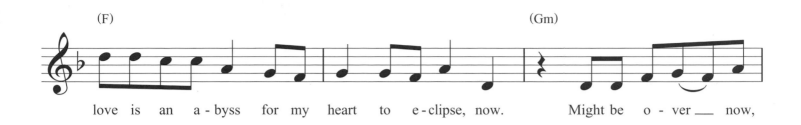

love is an a-byss for my heart to e-clipse, now. Might be o-ver ___ now,

but I feel it still.

Chorus

Ooh, _____ I'm a reb-el just for kicks, now.

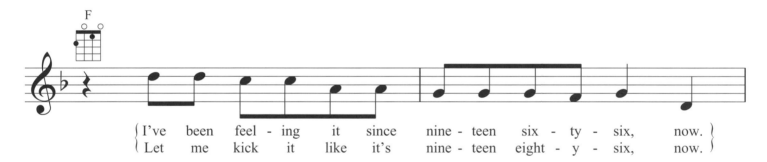

{ I've been feel-ing it since nine-teen six-ty-six, now. }
{ Let me kick it like it's nine-teen eight-y-six, now. }

1.

Might be o-ver ___ now, but I feel it still.

2.

Might have had your fill, but you feel it still. ___

Greatest Love Story

Words and Music by Brandon Lancaster

We were gon - na be the great-est love sto - ry this town had ev - er seen.
We were gon - na be the great-est love sto - ry this town had ev - er seen.
We're _ gon - na be the great-est love sto - ry this town has ev - er seen.

To Coda

1.

2. So,

2.

3. So,

Verse

you came back ____ af - ter a long four years. Your

col - lege boy - friend did - n't work out. ____ So, we went out ___ for a

cou - ple of drinks _ to find out who we are now. ____

20

Sure, we changed, _ but way deep down, _ you had the same old feel-ings for me. _

_ I went to the store and bought _ you a ring _ and I

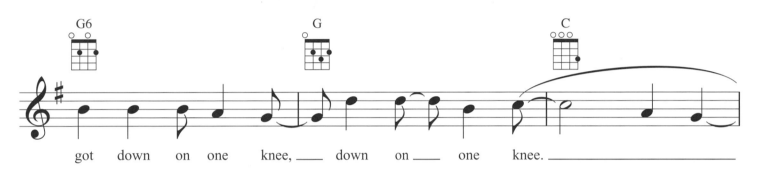

got down on one knee, _ down on _ one knee. _

D.S. al Coda

And I _ said:

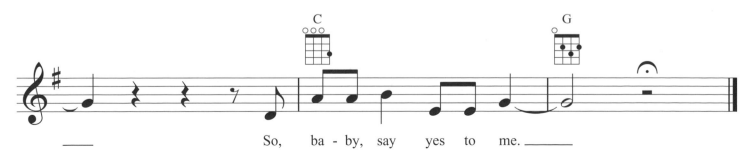

Outro
Coda

We're gon-na be the great-est love sto-ry this world has ev-er seen. _

_ So, ba-by, say yes to me. _

Havana

Words and Music by Camila Cabello, Louis Bell, Pharrell Williams,
Adam Feeney, Ali Tamposi, Brian Lee, Andrew Wotman,
Brittany Hazzard, Jeffery Lamar Williams and Brandon Perry

D.S. al Coda

And then I had to tell him I had to go, ___ oh, na na na na na. Ha-

Coda

Bridge

van - a, Ha - van - a, ooh na na. *(See additional lyrics)*

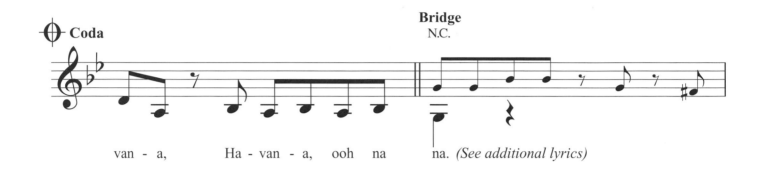

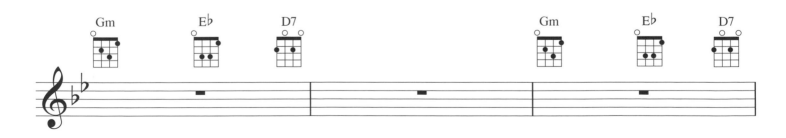

Outro

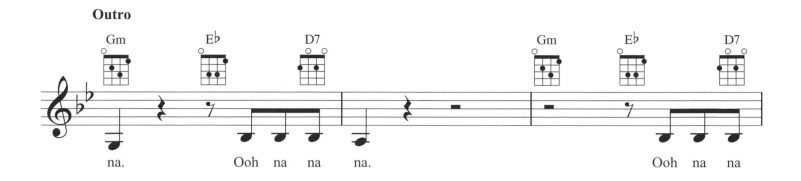

na.   Ooh na na na.   Ooh na na

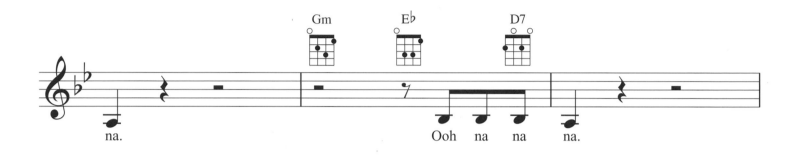

na.   Ooh na na na.

Ooh na na na.   Ha - van - a, ooh na na.

Additional Lyrics

Jeffery,
Just graduated, fresh on campus, mmm.
Fresh out East Atlanta with no manners, damn.
Fresh out East Atlanta.
Bump on her bumper like a traffic jam (jam).
Hey, I was quick to pay that girl like Uncle Sam. (Here you go, ay).
Back it on me, shawty cravin' on me.
Get to diggin' on me (on me).
She waited on me. (Then what?)
Shawty cakin' on me, got the bacon on me. (Wait up.)
This is history in the makin' on me (on me).
Point blank, close range, that be.
If it cost a million, that's me (that's me).
I was gettin' mula, man, they feel me.

Issues

Words and Music by Benjamin Levin, Mikkel Eriksen,
Tor Hermansen, Julia Michaels and Justin Tranter

First note

Verse
Moderately

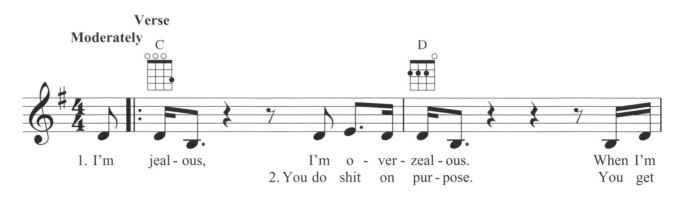

1. I'm   jeal - ous,   I'm o - ver - zeal - ous.   When I'm
2. You do shit on pur - pose.   You get

down, I get real down.   When I'm high, I don't come down.   I get
mad and you break things.   Feel __ bad, try to fix things.   But you're a

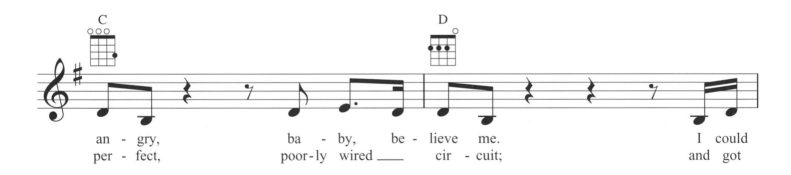

an - gry,   ba - by, be - lieve me.   I could
per - fect,   poor - ly wired __ cir - cuit;   and got

love you just like   that,   and I could leave you just as   fast.   But
hands like an o - cean,   push you   out, pull you back in.   'Cause

Pre-Chorus

you don't _ judge me. _ 'Cause if you did, ba - by, I would judge you,

too. No, you don't _ judge me. _ { 'Cause if you
{ 'Cause you

did, ba - by, I would judge you, too. } 'Cause I got is -
see it from the same point of view. }

𝄋 Chorus

- sues, but you got 'em, too. _____ So give 'em all _

_____ to me _ and I'll _ give mine _ to you. _____ Bask in the glo -

29

-ry of all our prob - lems, 'cause we got —

—— the kind — of love — it takes — to solve — 'em. Yeah, I got is-

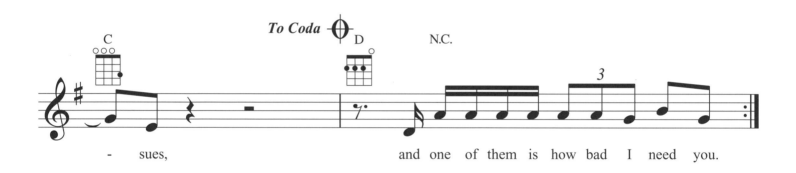

To Coda

- sues, and one of them is how bad I need you.

Bridge

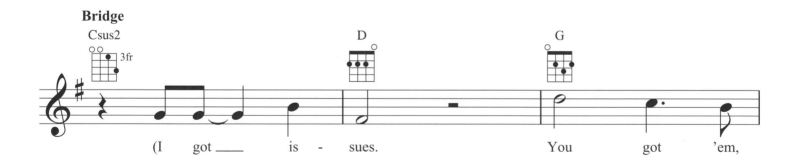

(I got —— is - sues. You got 'em,

too.) And one of them is how bad I need you. (I got —— is -

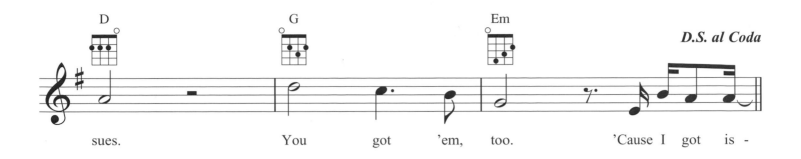

D.S. al Coda

sues. You got 'em, too. 'Cause I got is -

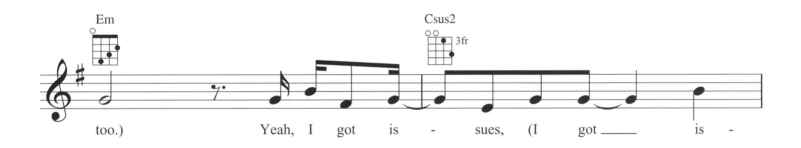

Coda **Outro**

and one of them is how bad I need you. (You got 'em,

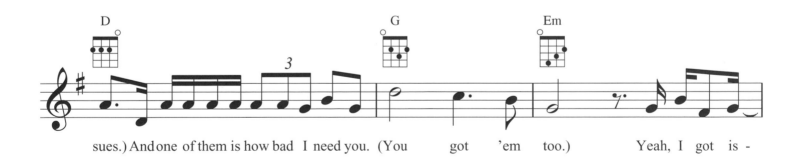

too.) Yeah, I got is - sues, (I got _____ is -

sues.) And one of them is how bad I need you. (You got 'em too.) Yeah, I got is -

- sues, (I got,) _____ and one of them is how bad I need you.

Location

Words and Music by Khalid Robinson, Joshua Scruggs, Samuel Jimenez,
Chris McClenney, Olatunji Ige, Alfredo Gonzalez and Barjam Kurti

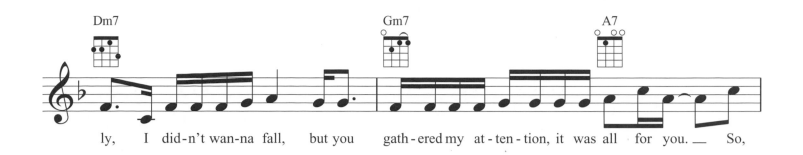

Dm7   Gm7   A7

ly,   I did-n't wan-na fall,   but you   gath-ered my at-ten-tion, it was all   for you. __ So,

B♭maj7   A7

don't   take ad-van - tage, don't leave my heart dam - aged. I un-der-stand __

Dm7   C   F+

__ that things _ go a lit-tle bit bet-ter when you plan it.   Oh, __ so won't you send __

𝄋 **Chorus**

B♭maj7   A7

__ me   your lo - ca - tion, let's   fo - cus on com - mu - ni - cat - in' 'cause

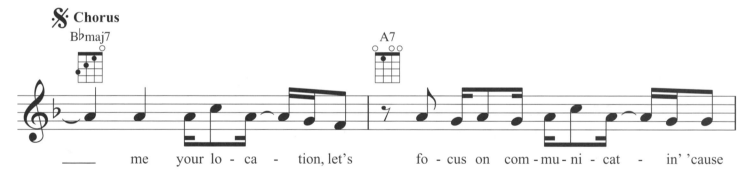

Dm7   Gm7

I just need __ the time and place _ to come through.

2nd time only: (Chance _ to come through.) _____

B♭maj7   A7

Send   me   your lo - ca - tion, let's   ride   the vi - bra - tions.

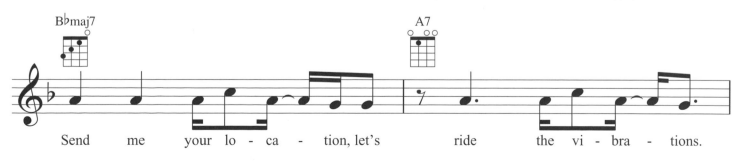

Perfect

Words and Music by Ed Sheeran

time. _____ Dar - ling, just kiss me slow, your heart is
time. _____ Dar - ling, just hold my hand. Be my girl, I'll

all ____ I ____ own. And in your eyes, you're ____ hold - ing mine. _
be ____ your ____ man. I've seen the fu - ture ____ in your eyes. _

Chorus

___ } Ba - by, _____ I'm danc - ing in the

dark with you be - tween my arms. Bare - foot on the

grass, lis - ten - ing to our ___ fa - v'rite song. { When you said you looked a
{ When I saw you in that

To Coda

mess, I whis - pered un - der - neath my breath. But you heard it, "Dar - ling,
dress, look - ing so beau - ti - ful, I don't ___ de - serve this. "Dar - ling,

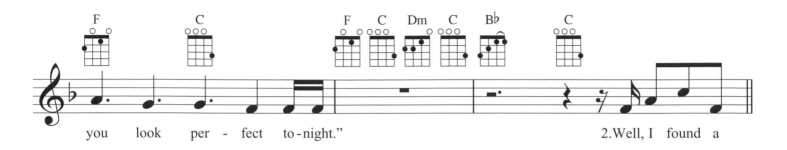

you look per - fect to - night." 2.Well, I found a

Verse

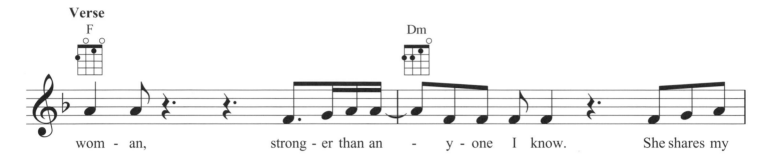

wom - an, strong - er than an - y - one I know. She shares my

dreams; I hope _ that some-day I'll share her home. _____ I found a love _

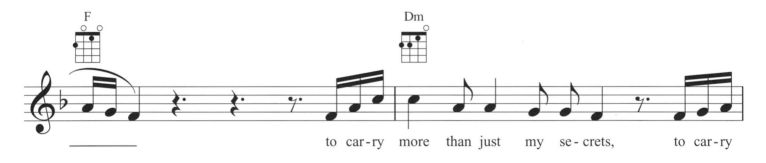

_____ to car-ry more than just my se-crets, to car-ry

D.S. al Coda

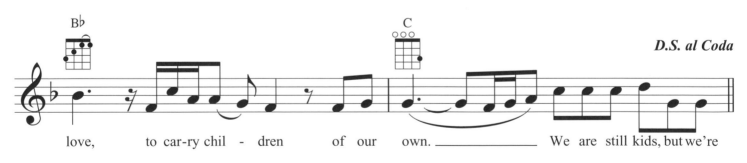

love, to car-ry chil - dren of our own. _____ We are still kids, but we're

Coda **Interlude**

you look per - fect to - night."

Outro-Chorus

Ba - by, _____ I'm _____ danc - ing in the

dark with you be - tween my arms. Bare - foot on the

grass, lis - ten - ing to our __ fa - v'rite song. I have faith in what _ I

see. Now I know I have met an an - gel in per - son, and

she looks per - fect. I don't de - serve this, you look per - fect to-night.

Praying

Words and Music by Kesha Sebert, Ben Abraham, Ryan Lewis and Andrew Joslyn

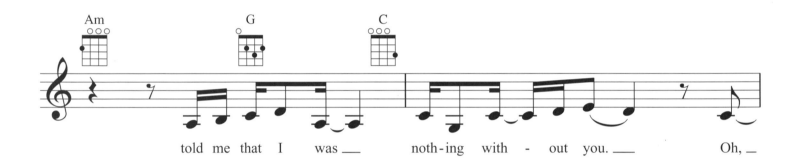

1. Well, you al - most had me fooled;

told me that I was noth - ing with - out you. Oh,

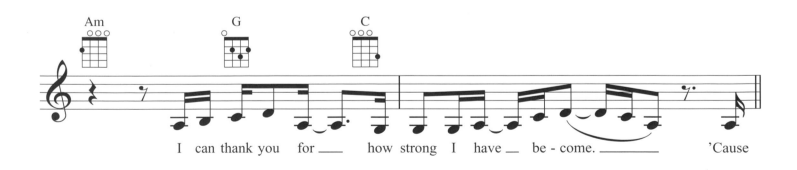

but af - ter ev - 'ry - thing you've done,

I can thank you for how strong I have be - come. 'Cause

42

Sorry Not Sorry

Words and Music by Demitria Lovato, Sean Douglas,
Warren Felder, William Simmons and Trevor Brown

First note

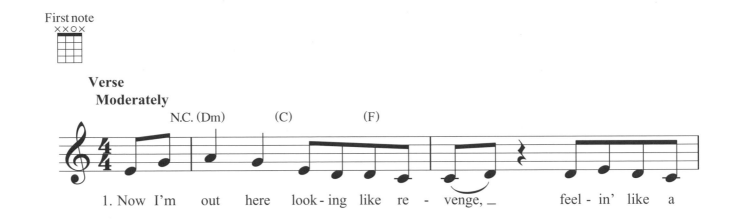

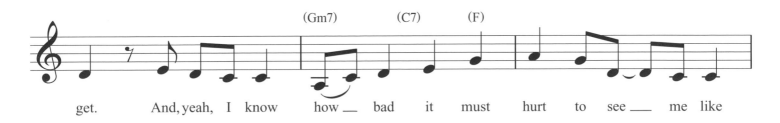

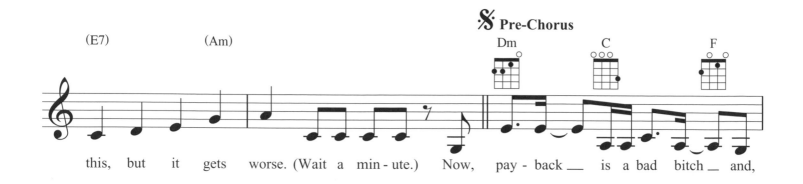

this, but it gets worse. (Wait a min - ute.) Now, pay - back __ is a bad bitch __ and,

ba - by, __ I'm the bad - est. __ You f**k - in' __ with a sav - age, __ can't

have __ this, __ can't have __ this. __ And it be

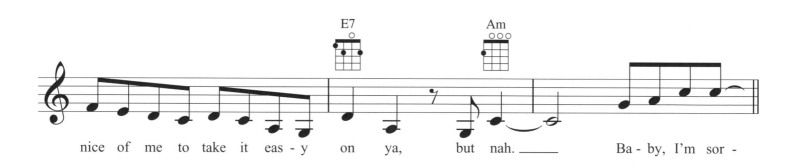

nice of me to take it eas - y on ya, but nah. _____ Ba - by, I'm sor -

𝄋 𝄋 Chorus

- ry. (I'm not sor - ry.) Ba - by, I'm sor - ry. (I'm not

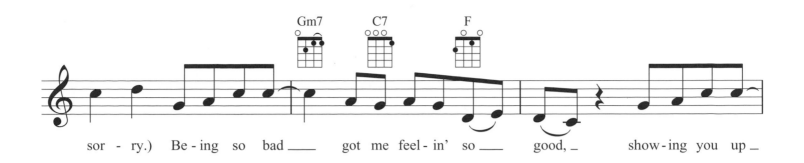

sor - ry.) Be - ing so bad ___ got me feel - in' so ___ good, _ show-ing you up _

___ like I knew that I would. _ Ba - by, I'm sor - ry. (I'm not

sor - ry.) Ba - by, I'm sor - ry. (I'm not sor - ry.) Feel - ing in - spi -

To Coda 1
To Coda 2

- red 'cause the ta - bles have _ turned. _ Yeah, I'm on fi - re and I know that it ___

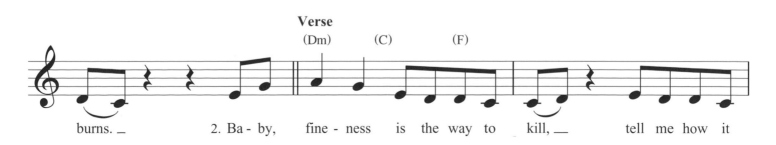

Verse
(Dm)   (C)   (F)

burns. _   2. Ba - by, fine - ness is the way to kill, _ tell me how it

feel, but it's such a bit - ter pill. __ And, yeah, I know you __ thought you had

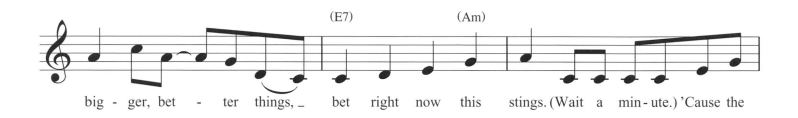

big - ger, bet - ter things, __ bet right now this stings. (Wait a min - ute.) 'Cause the

grass is green - er un - der me, __ bright as tech - ni - col - or, I can tell that you can

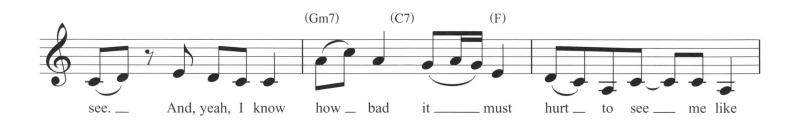

see. __ And, yeah, I know how __ bad it _____ must hurt __ to see ___ me like

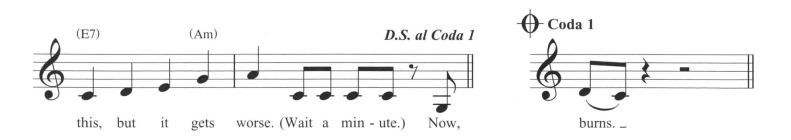

this, but it gets worse. (Wait a min - ute.) Now, burns. __

Bridge

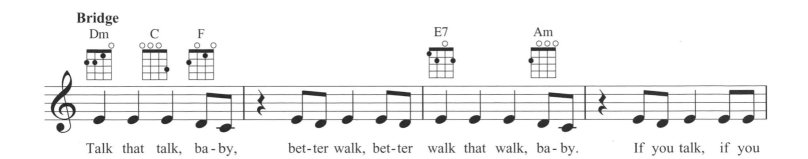

Talk that talk, ba-by, bet-ter walk, bet-ter walk that walk, ba-by. If you talk, if you

talk __ that talk, ba-by, bet-ter walk, bet-ter walk that walk, ba-by. Oh, _____ yeah,

talk that talk, ba-by, bet-ter walk, __ bet-ter walk that __ walk, ba-by.

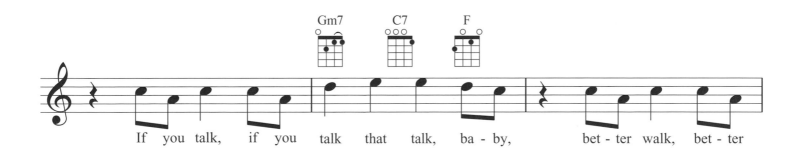

If you talk, if you talk that talk, ba-by, bet-ter walk, bet-ter

D.S.S. al Coda 2   **Coda 2**

walk that walk, ba-by.   Ba-by, I'm sor-   burns. __

Redbone

Words and Music by Donald Glover, Ludwig Goransson,
George Clinton, William Collins and Gary Cooper

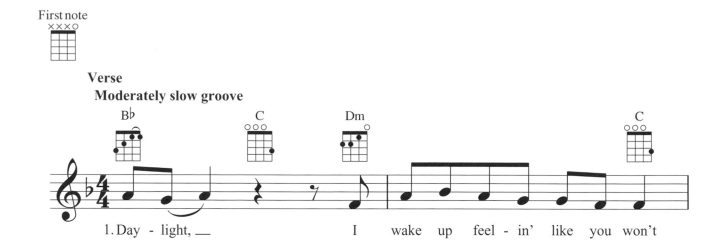

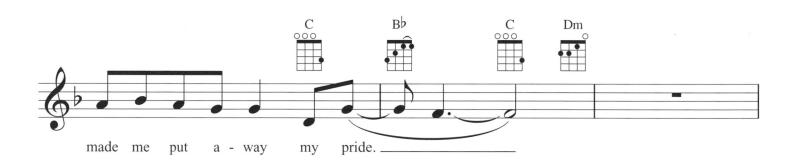

make it hard for a boy like that to go on. ___ I'm wish-in' I could make this mine, ___

Pre-Chorus

N.C.

___ oh. ___ If you want it, you can

have it. If you need it, we can make it, oh. _____ If ___

Chorus

___ you want ___ it, you can have it. But stay woke, nig-gas

creep-in'. They gon' find you, gon' catch you sleep-in'. Ooh, ___ now stay woke,

To Coda

nig-gas creep-in'. Now, don't you close your eyes. ___

Verse

2. Too late, ___ you wan-na make it right, but now it's

too late. ___ My pea-nut but-ter choc-'late cake with Kool-Aid. ___ I'm

try-in' not to waste my time. _____ If you

Pre-Chorus

want it, you can have it. If you need it, we can

make it, oh. _____ If ___ you want ___ it, you can have it.

D.S. al Coda

But stay woke,

Coda

But stay woke,

Say Something

Words and Music by Justin Timberlake, Chris Stapleton, Nate Hills, Larrance Dopson and Tim Mosley

1. Ev-'ry-one knows all ___ a-bout

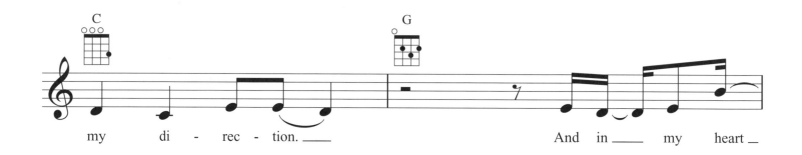

my di-rec-tion. ___ And in ___ my heart ___

___ some-where, _ I ___ wan-na go ___ there. Still, I ___ don't go ___

___ there. Ev-'ry-bod-y says, "Say ___ some-thing, say ___ some-thing,

say __ some - thing, say __ some - thing, say __ some - thing, say __ some - thing." __

Chorus

__ I don't wan - na get caught up in ___ the rhy-thm of it, but I ___ can't help ___ my - self. ___ No, I ___ can't help _

__ my - self, ___ no, no. Caught up in ___ the mid - dle of it. No, I ___ can't help ___ my - self. ___ No, I ___ can't help _

__ my - self, ___ no, no, no. __ Caught up in ___ the

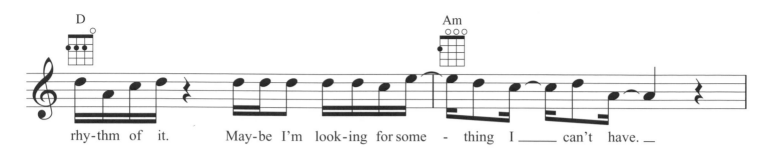

rhy-thm of it.   May-be I'm look-ing for some - thing I ___ can't have. __

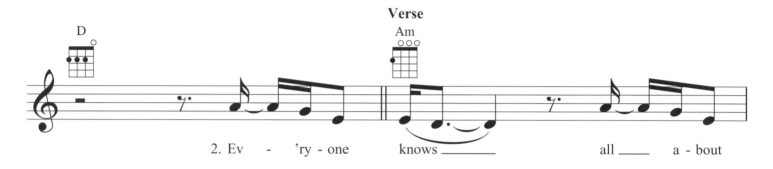

May - be I'm look-ing for some - thing I ___ can't ___ have.

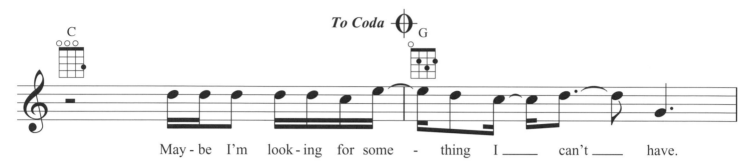

2. Ev - 'ry - one   knows ___   all ___ a - bout

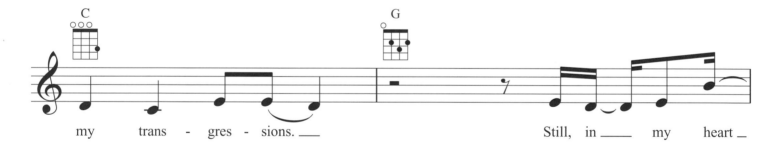

my   trans - gres - sions. ___   Still, in ___ my   heart __

___ some - where, _   there's   mel - o - dy   and

har - mo - ny   for   you   and   me   to - night. ___

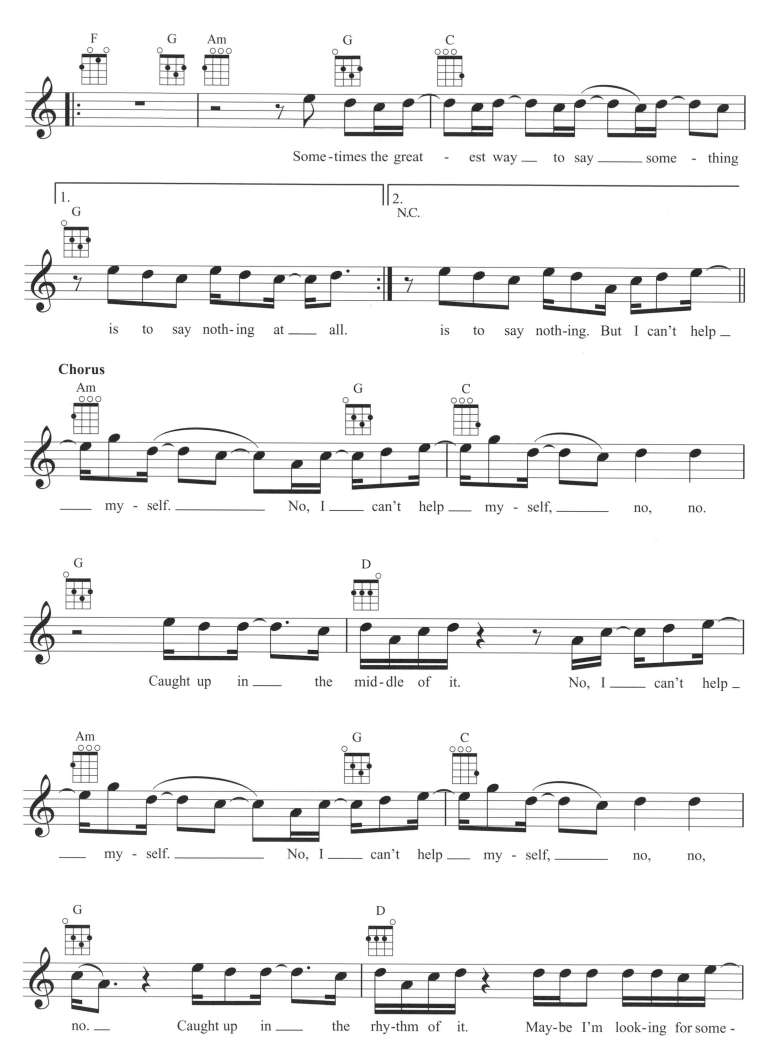

Some-times the great - est way — to say — some - thing

1. is to say noth-ing at — all.

2. is to say noth-ing. But I can't help —

Chorus

— my - self. — No, I — can't help — my - self, — no, no.

Caught up in — the mid-dle of it. No, I — can't help —

— my - self. — No, I — can't help — my - self, — no, no,

no. — Caught up in — the rhy-thm of it. May-be I'm look-ing for some -

There's Nothing Holdin' Me Back

Words and Music by Shawn Mendes, Geoffrey Warburton, Teddy Geiger and Scott Harris

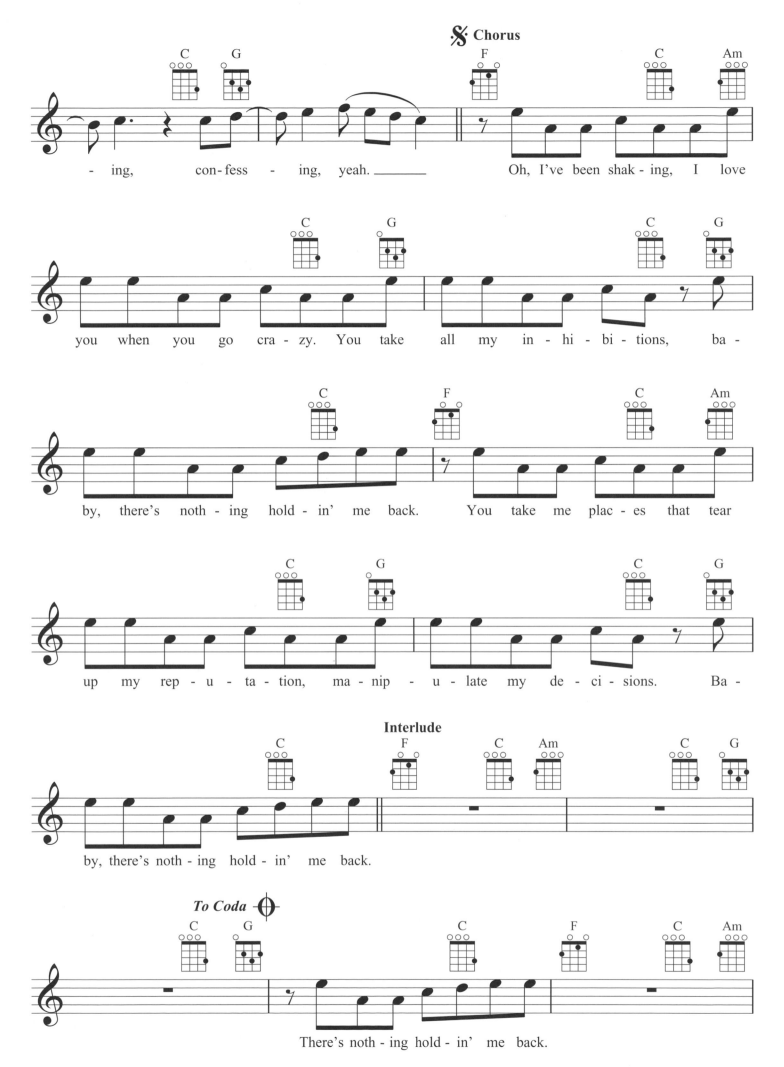

There's noth-ing hold-in' me back.

Bridge

'Cause if we lost our minds and we took __

__ it way too far, I know we'd be al-right, I know we __

__ would be al-right. If you were by my side and we stum-

-bled in the dark, I know we'd be al-right, I know we __

__ would be al-right. 'Cause if we lost our minds and we took __

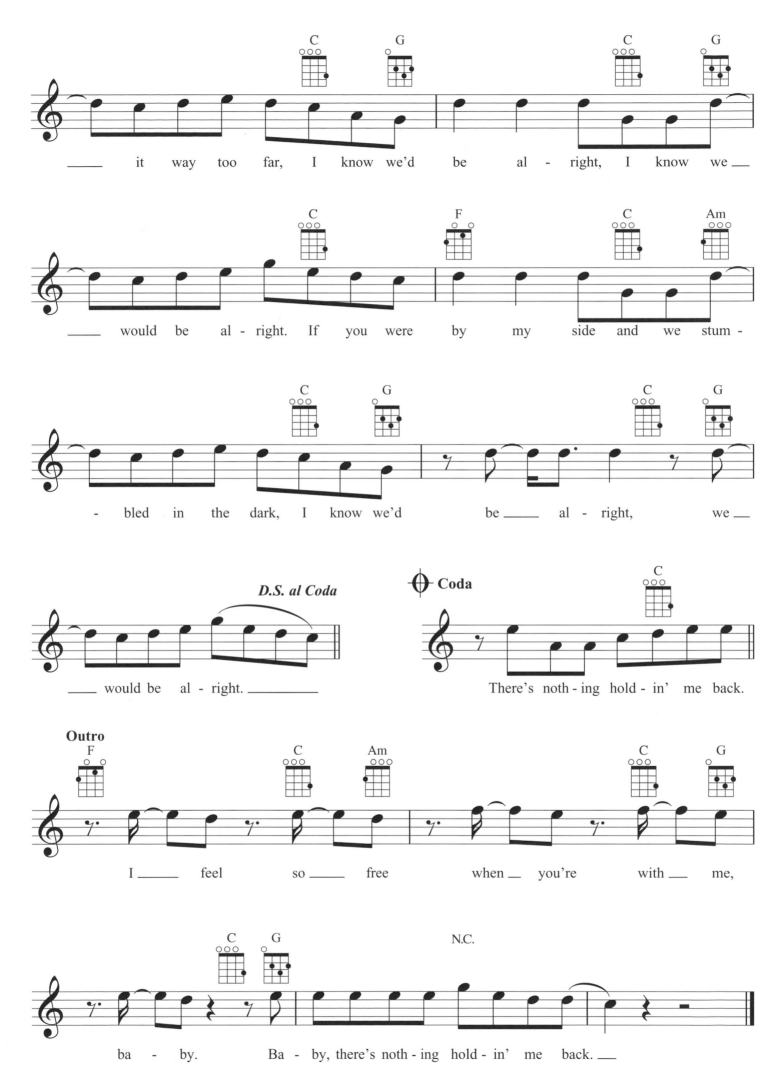

it way too far, I know we'd be al - right, I know we

would be al - right. If you were by my side and we stum -

- bled in the dark, I know we'd be al - right, we

D.S. al Coda

would be al - right.

Coda

There's noth - ing hold - in' me back.

Outro

I feel so free when you're with me,

ba - by. Ba - by, there's noth - ing hold - in' me back.

Thunder

**Words and Music by Dan Reynolds, Wayne Sermon, Ben McKee,
Daniel Platzman, Alexander Grant and Jayson DeZuzio**

1. Just a young gun with a quick fuse, I was up-tight, wan-na let loose.

I was dream-ing of big-ger things and want-na leave my own life be-hind.

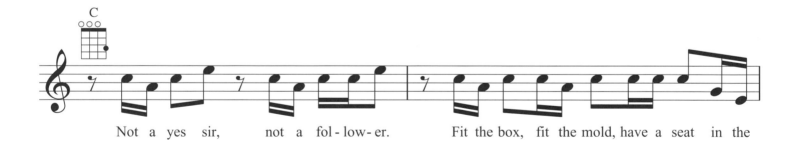

Not a yes sir, not a fol-low-er. Fit the box, fit the mold, have a seat in the

foy-er, take a num-ber. I was light-ning be-fore the thun-der, thun-der.

Thun - der, thun - der, thun, thun - der, thu - thu - thun - der, thun - der.

Thun - der, thun - der, thun, thun - der, thu - thu - thun - der, thun - der.

Thun - der, ___ feel the thun - der, ___ light - ning and the thun - der. ___

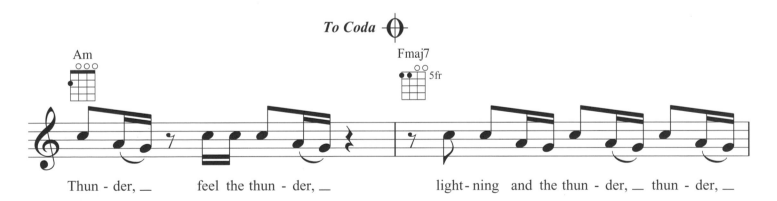

Thun - der, ___ feel the thun - der, ___ light - ning and the thun - der, ___ thun - der, ___

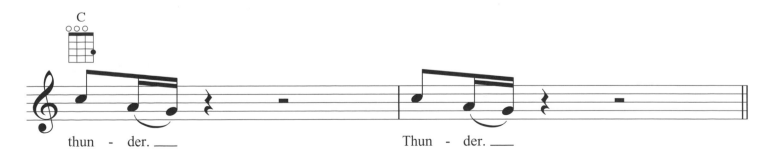

thun - der. ___ Thun - der. ___

Verse

C

2. Kids were laugh - ing   in my class - es   while I was schem - ing   for the mass - es.

F

"Who do you think __ you are _____   dream - ing 'bout be - ing a big __ star?" _____

C

You say you're bas - ic,   you say you're eas - y,   you're al - ways rid - ing   in the back seat.

Fmaj7

D.S. al Coda

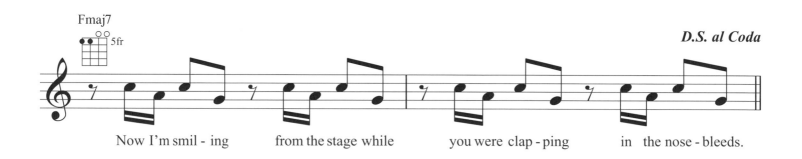

Now I'm smil - ing   from the stage while   you were clap - ping   in the nose - bleeds.

Coda

Fmaj7

light - ning   and the thun - der, _____   thun - der. _____

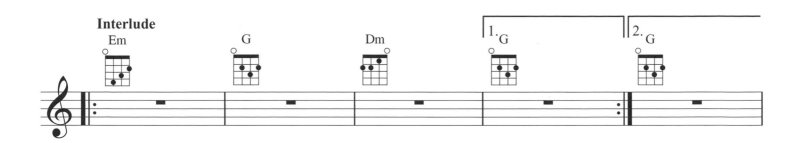

Interlude

N.C.

Thun - der, __ feel the thun - der, __ light - ning and the thun - der, __ thun - der. __

Chorus

C

Thun - der, __ feel the thun - der, __ light-ning and the thun - der, __ thun - der. __

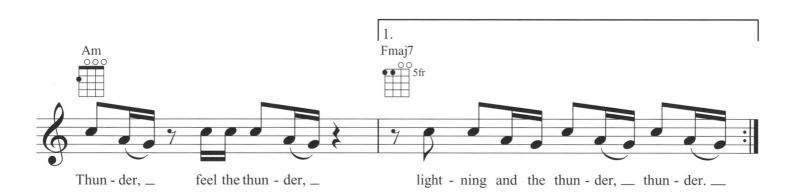

Am | 1. Fmaj7

Thun - der, __ feel the thun - der, __ light - ning and the thun - der, __ thun - der. __

2. Fmaj7 | C

light - ning and the thun - der, ___ thun - der. ___

Too Good at Goodbyes

Words and Music by Sam Smith, Tor Hermansen,
Mikkel Eriksen and James Napier

1. You must think that I'm stu - pid.
2. I know you're think - ing I'm heart - less.

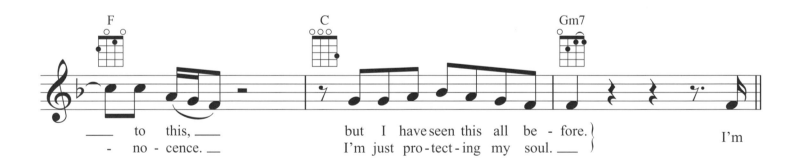

You must think that I'm a fool. _____ You must think that I'm new —
I know you're think - ing I'm cold. _____ I'm just pro - tect - ing my in -

_____ to this, ___ but I have seen this all be - fore.⎫ I'm
- no - cence. __ I'm just pro - tect - ing my soul. __ ⎭

Pre-Chorus

nev - er gon - na let you close to me, e - ven though you mean the most to me. 'Cause

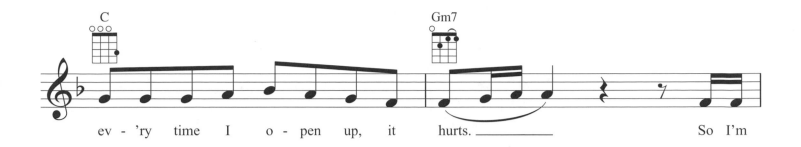

ev-'ry time I o-pen up, it hurts. _____ So I'm

nev-er gon-na get too close to you, e - ven when I mean the most to you, in

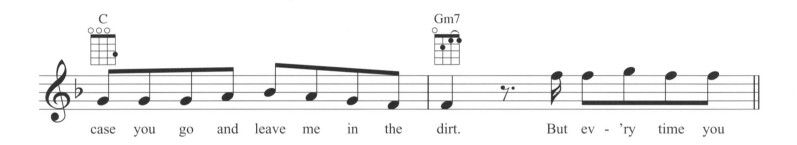

case you go and leave me in the dirt. But ev-'ry time you

𝄋 Chorus

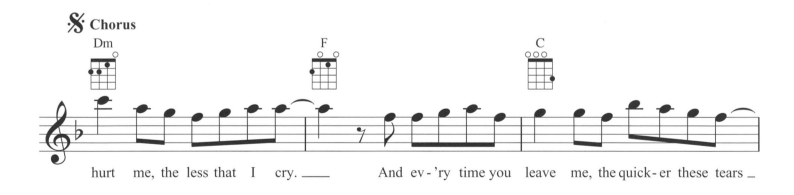

hurt me, the less that I cry. ____ And ev-'ry time you leave me, the quick-er these tears _

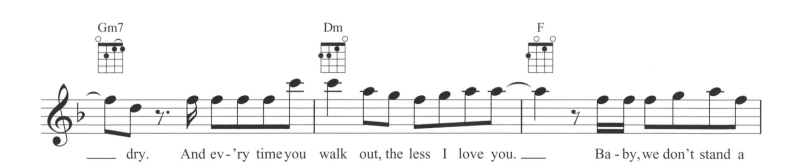

____ dry. And ev-'ry time you walk out, the less I love you. ____ Ba-by, we don't stand a

chance;   it's sad but it's true. ___ I'm way too good at good-byes. ___ (I'm way too good at good - byes.)

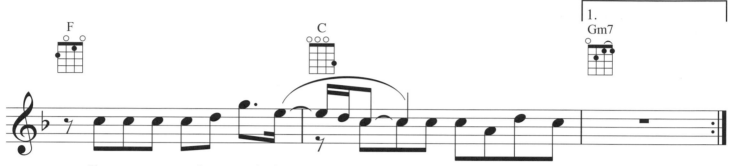

1.

I'm way too good at good - byes. _____
(I'm   way too good at good - byes.)

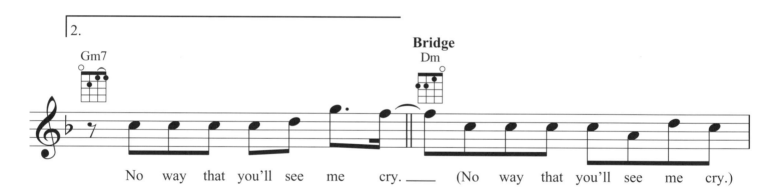

2.

Bridge

No   way   that   you'll   see   me   cry. ___ (No   way   that   you'll   see   me   cry.)

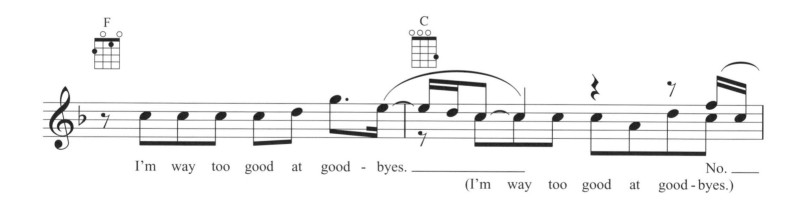

I'm   way   too   good   at   good - byes. _____   No. ___
(I'm   way   too   good   at   good - byes.)

___   (I'm   way   too   good   at   good - byes.)
          (No   way   that   you'll   see   me   cry.)

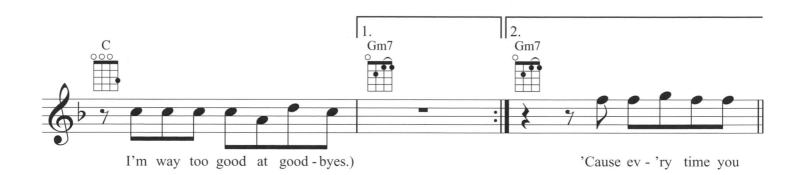

I'm way too good at good-byes.)

'Cause ev-'ry time you

Outro-Chorus

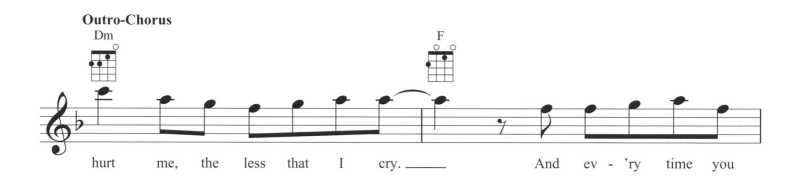

hurt me, the less that I cry. ____ And ev-'ry time you

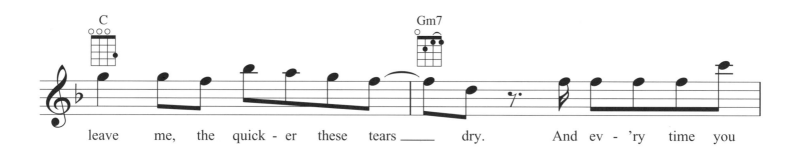

leave me, the quick-er these tears ____ dry. And ev-'ry time you

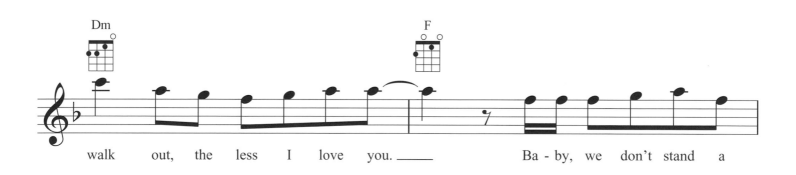

walk out, the less I love you. ____ Ba-by, we don't stand a

chance; it's sad but it's true. ___ I'm way too good at good-byes. ___

What Lovers Do

**Words and Music by Adam Levine, Solana Rowe, Jason Evigan,
Oladayo Olatunji, Brittany Hazzard, Victor Raadstrom and Ben Diehl**

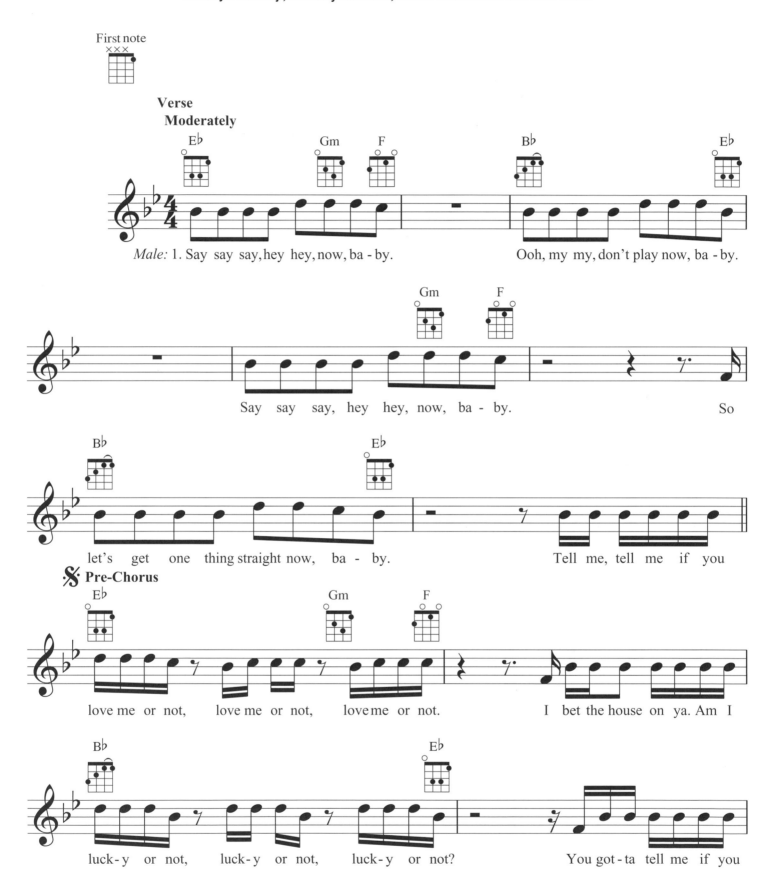

love me or not, love me or not, love me or not. Been wish-ing for ya. Am I

luck - y or not, luck - y or not, luck - y or not?

Chorus

Ooh ooh ooh ooh ooh, __ been wish - ing for you, __ ooh, __ ooh, __ try - na do what

lov - ers do, __ ooh. __ Ooh ooh ooh ooh ooh, __ been wish - ing for you, __ ooh, __

To Coda ⊕

Verse

ooh, __ try - na do what lov - ers do, __ ooh. __ 2. Say say say, hey hey, now, ba - by.

Female:

You gon' make me hit you with that lay down, ba - by.

Male: (Oh, ____ ____ say say say, hey hey, now, ba - by.)

Oh, ____ say say say, hey hey, now, ba - by,

D.S. al Coda

You know what I need out the gate, now, ba - by.   Male: Tell me, tell me if you

Coda   Interlude

lov - ers do, ___ ooh. ___   What lov - ers do.

1.   2.

What lov - ers do. ___

Bridge

Male: Aren't we too grown for games?   Aren't we too grown to play a - round?

Young e - nough to chase, but old e - nough _ to know bet - ter.   Female: Are we too grown for chang - in'?

What About Us

Words and Music by Alecia Moore, Steve Mac and Johnny McDaid

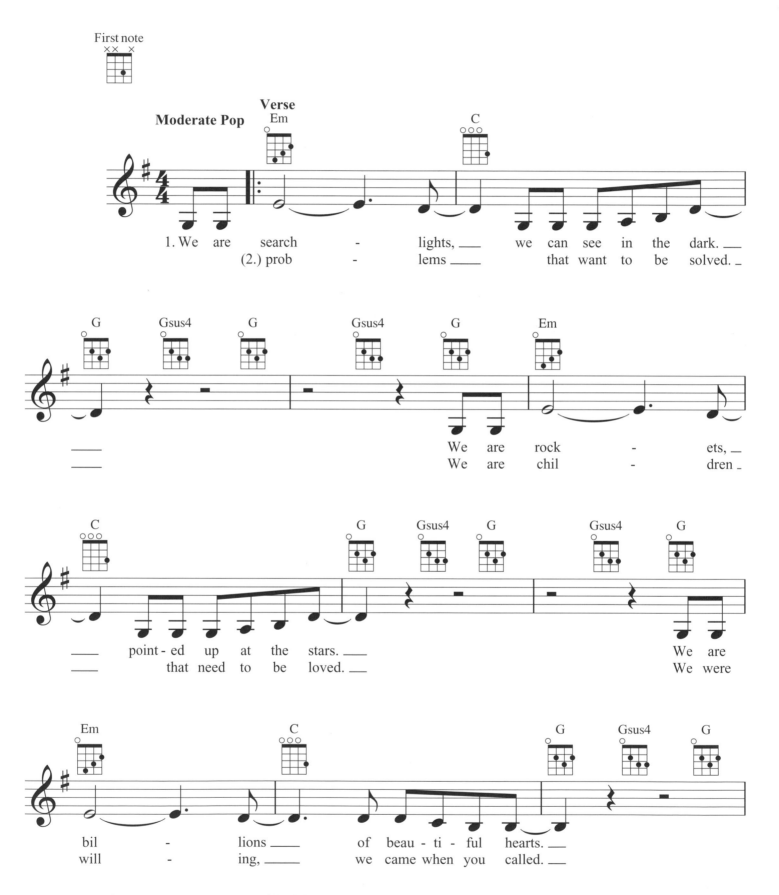

And you sold _____ us _____ down the riv - er too far. _____
But, man, you fooled _____ us; _____ e - nough is e - nough. _

Chorus

What a - bout us? What a - bout

all the times you said you had the an - swers? What a - bout

us? What a - bout all the bro - ken hap - py ev - er

af - ters? What a - bout us? What a - bout

To Coda

all the plans that end - ed in dis - as - ter? _____